£3

Out of the Depths

Out of the Depths

PRAYERS OF HOPE TO RAISE UP THE BROKEN

Elizabeth Babbs

eagle

Guildford, Surrey

Other titles by Elizabeth Babbs:

Can God Help M.E? (book)
Come and Rest (audio tape and CD)

Copyright © 2001 Eagle Publishing

British Library Cataloguing in Publication Data.
A catalogue record for this book is available from the British
Library.

Published by Eagle Publishing PO Box 530, Guildford, Surrey
GU2 4FH.

Scripture quotations are taken from the *Holy Bible, New
International Version.* Copyright © 1973, 1978, 1984 by
International Bible Society (used by permission of Hodder &
Stoughton, a Division of Hodder Headline). Those marked NLT
are from the *Holy Bible, New Living Translation.* Copyright ©
Tyndale House.

Picture credits: pp.6–7 © Antony Edwards; pp. 28–29, © John C.
Dorrnkamp; pp. 20, 36, 44–45, © Janey Napier

Typeset by Eagle
Printed in Hong Kong
ISBN No: 0 86347 405 5

Contents

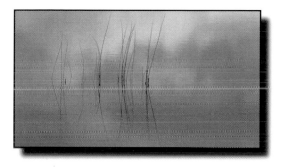

OUT OF THE DEPTHS
I CRY TO YOU,
O LORD;
O LORD, HEAR MY VOICE.

PSALM 130:1

PART ONE

Where are
You Lord?

O N E

Lord, it feels like You've left me
Have You abandoned me?
Do You hate me?
Where are You Lord?

Is this as good as it gets?
No end in sight
Just endless hours
rolled into long dark days.

Where is Your truth?
What are Your promises?
Where is the hope for my life?

My child, you are everything to me

How could you think otherwise?
I feel what you are going through
and it grieves me too.
Only I can see the full picture –
from eternity back to this present
moment in time.
Allow me to comfort you
to bind up your wounds
and bring restoration and healing
to the depths of your being.

T W O

Lord, I don't know how to live
with this uncertainty
Fear gnawing at the root of trust
And the not knowing paralyses me.
Where are You Lord?
What is happening to me?
How can I go on?

My child,
Never will I leave you
Never will I forsake you.
I'm always here for you
watching, waiting, listening, loving,
I will never let you go.

T H R E E

Lord, I want to avert my gaze from You
I'm ashamed to come into Your presence.
Help me to stop hiding
Reassure me of Your love
and melt the icy tentacles that grip within.
Unchain my spirit
and allow Your truth to penetrate
so that I can stand complete in You.

My dear one
you are a child of God
don't shrink behind other people.
Shine as children do.
Be liberated from your fear
and know that I lovingly created you
as my own personal treasure.

Lord, I'm sick of being told
that Your light extinguishes the darkness
Where is the light?

I live in the land of the shadow of death
Not a single shaft of light illuminates
the exit to this personal prison.

When will You call me out of this place?

My precious child
I haven't forgotten you
I'm holding you securely
in the palm of my hand.
My child I know that you are angry
I can feel that pain and hurt within.
Let me take it from you
it's my load to bear not yours
For I am the God of justice and mercy.

FIVE

Lord, it's hopeless
Everything useless
Discarded on the scrap heap of those who can't.
What do I have left to live for?
Life so pointless
purposeless
redundant.
Locked in pain
Imprisoned by fear
Can't someone tell me Why?

My child,
know that I love you
know too that I care.
Can you love me
even if I never tell you why?
I'm calling you deeper –
into total dependency.
Take your identity from me
drawing every breath from mine
then you will find value and meaning.

S I X

Trapped in the wilderness of my emotions
my heart set like rock
I've turned away from You Lord
and have lost everything.
Lord, help me to cry out to You again
and release me from condemnation.
Flood my mind with images of beauty and colour.
Shelter me, protect me and release me
I want to find myself in You once more.

My child,

the darkness can't obscure my colours
it only serves to highlight their radiance.
Colours may be glimpsed
and then seem to vanish
but my love is blended in beauty.
Remember the rainbow –
My promise that I will never leave you
nor forsake you.
Nothing can eclipse my love for you –
It's the light that shines
the pathway from here to eternity.

15

Locked inside the prison walls of desperation
Confronted by failure at every turn
Paralysed with grief
My cry "How Long?"
Echoes through this carpet of nothingness.

I love you my child
and long to nourish your roots.
Don't resist, but instead yield
and as you send your roots down deeper into me
I will sustain you
Nothing will harm you.
You are my precious child
in whom I delight.

E I G H T

They say that time is a great healer
But for me it's an endless suffocating void
echoing Your absence
Not Your presence.

I'm here with you my child
right beside you.
I created this world
so that we could enjoy it together.
Can't you hear my voice echoing through creation?
Yes, creation groans and travails too
but my beauty can never be overshadowed.
It's your company I desire more than anything else.
That is the only sacrifice I am calling you to –
To spend time with me.

Where is Your gift of life?
That saving grace
You poured Yourself out to give.
And where do love and sorrow meet?
Lord, help me to make sense of this nothingness.

My child,
I gave you a gift beyond measure
and have nothing left to give.
For my life was poured out
through the death of my Son.
Such is my love for you.

PART TWO

Letting Go

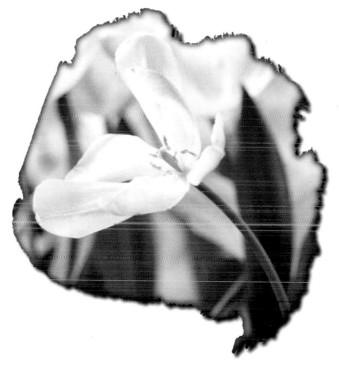

DON'T BE AFRAID,

FOR I AM WITH YOU.

DO NOT BE DISMAYED,

FOR I AM YOUR GOD.

I WILL STRENGTHEN YOU.

I WILL HELP YOU.

I WILL UPHOLD YOU WITH MY

VICTORIOUS RIGHT HAND.

ISAIAH 41:10 (NLT)

O N E

Lord, in the darkness and uncertainty of not knowing
I tentatively reach out my hand of faith to You
Trusting in a God who is able to transform all things
And whose light penetrates even this present darkness.

T W O

I didn't realise how much
I needed to hear the words
that You haven't forgotten me.
I've been abandoned by so many friends,
people who said they cared.
The disappointment
the isolation
the sense of abandonment.
Lord, it hurts!

T H R E E

Lord, help me to forgive.
For only forgiveness
can release me from the prison of the past
and cause a gateway of hope
to emerge from the rubble of my feelings
so that peace can be reborn.

F O U R

Lord, as the sun breaks through the darkness
and the warm shafts of light beckon me to bathe
Help me to uncurl
to yield
to let go.

24

F I V E

Lord, I'm waiting . . .
And in the waiting
I surrender all that I am to You
Knowing that You have been waiting
for this precise moment.

S I X

Lord, re-energise my spirit
and pour new life into me.
Allow the abundance of Your love
to flow through me
so that it brims over to others.

S E V E N

Lord, I don't feel much like praying today
But I am comforted by the knowledge
that I remain in Your thoughts all day long . . .
Such is my preciousness to You!
And so I allow myself simply to be
to rest
and to let go . . .

E I G H T

Lord, in faith I thank You
Because thanking You
Releases more of the fragrance
of Your presence
into my life.

N I N E

I am here Lord
Don't let go of me
But draw me closer . . .
For without You
I have nothing.

PART THREE

Come and Rest

COME WITH ME BY YOURSELVES

TO A QUIET PLACE AND GET

SOME REST.

MARK 6:31

O N E

Lord, the flame of my being is all but snuffed out
Breathe new life into me
Rekindle my hope and
Re-ignite this cowering flame.

T W O

Lord, Your rhythm
Not my rhythm
Your footprints
Not mine.

Retune my heart
Restore that still centre within
and meet me Lord in that secret place
where nothing matters except You.

T H R E E

Lord, as I still myself before You
I know that only You can quieten the churnings within
and calm the storm of my being.
Yet somehow Lord I trust –
Trust in a God who is much greater
than the sum of my feelings
Who reaches down into the dark weariness of my soul
So that peace can be reborn.

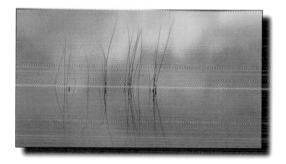

Renew me Lord
and bring Your healing and forgiveness.

Refresh me Lord
and bring life into the staleness of my existence
fresh hope in disillusionment.

Release me Lord from this numbing pain
and help me to feel the warmth
of Your love again.

F I V E

In the silence
I offer myself to You.
Help me to be open and receptive
as You speak to me.
Quieten my body
Still my mind
so that I may truly commune with You
and soak up the gift of Your presence.

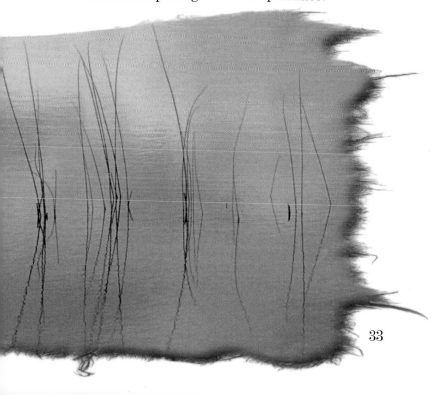

Lord, open my ears to hear You
Release my heart to touch You
Renew my vision
Transform my situation
Help me to see the impression
of Your footprints across my life . . .
Transforming
Redeeming
Restoring
Revealing.

Lord, I thank you that You are my Shepherd
That You lead me and guide me.
Even when I'm far away from You
You look after me, supplying all my needs.

You give me strength when I feel like giving up
and make mountains into level paths for me.
You lead me beside tranquil waters
and provide rest and refreshment
for my whole being.

PART FOUR

Such Love

FOR I AM CONVINCED THAT
NEITHER DEATH NOR LIFE,
NEITHER ANGELS NOR DEMONS,
NEITHER THE PRESENT NOR THE
FUTURE, NOR ANY POWERS,
NEITHER HEIGHT NOR DEPTH, NOR
ANYTHING ELSE IN ALL CREATION,
WILL BE ABLE TO SEPARATE US
FROM THE LOVE OF GOD THAT IS IN
CHRIST JESUS OUR LORD.

(ROMANS 8:38 & 39)

O N E

Lord, You look beyond my failings and see my needs
You reach out to me
Clasping me victoriously.
You walk ahead of me through the pain
And stoop down to cover me.
And Lord, when I can walk no further
You carry me.

T W O

From the depths of my fears
You quench my soul with Your tears
You hold me
You enfold me
I'm secure in Your arms.

T H R E E

Lord, You found me at the lowest point in my life
Unable to go on
Unable to function.
You saw rejection as an open door
And walked with me unravelling this shroud of grief
Gently touching my heart
And releasing me from captivity.

F O U R

Such love pours itself out for me
Such love accepts me as I am
Such love heals my brokenness
Such love flows through me to others.

F I V E

Lord, Your love supports
strengthens
enfolds

Binds up the broken hearted
Touches the point of pain
Gives grace to forgive.

S I X

Lord, I am a precious jewel in Your crown
Honed in Your image
Ground in love to perfection
Seated at the right hand of God
I belong to You.

S E V E N

Lord, Your faithfulness
cancels out my sense of worthlessness
I am significant because You made me
Crafted from love
I am Your work of art.

E I G H T

Lord, in the darkness of unknowing . . . You come.
In the silence and the waiting . . . You come.
In the midst of pain and suffering . . . You come.
Lord, You Come to my Rescue.

PART FIVE

Beauty from Ashes

TO ALL WHO MOURN IN ISRAEL,

HE WILL GIVE BEAUTY FOR ASHES,

JOY INSTEAD OF MOURNING,

PRAISE INSTEAD OF DESPAIR.

FOR THE LORD HAS PLANTED THEM

LIKE STRONG AND GRACEFUL OAKS

FOR HIS OWN GLORY.

(ISAIAH 61:3 NLT)

O N E

Lord, I found You in a place of utter despair
and from that moment onwards everything changed.
You reached down to me when no one else could
and began to transform the shadows of my past
into something beautiful.
Even my brokenness is a precious gift to You.

T W O

Lord, thank You that You use suffering
to shine a pathway to You
Drawn into closer communion
I'm secure in the knowledge that
Your presence will NEVER leave me

T H R E E

Beauty from ashes
Hope for despair
Your arm stretched towards me
When no one was there.

Light in my darkness
Strength to overcome
You lead me to victory
The battle is won.

I praise You my Father
For You answer prayer
Your faithfulness reigns
I'm released from despair.

F O U R

Lord, I thank You
For You have turned
My pain and suppression
Into Your Glorious Expression.

```
        H
BUT FOUND IN
        P
        E
        L
    YOU
        S
        T
```